Growing Giant Pumpkins – How To Grow Massive Pumpkins At Home

Jason Johns

Visit me at www.OwningAnAllotment.com for gardening tips and advice or follow me at www.YouTube.com/OwningAnAllotment for my video diary and tips. Join me on Facebook at www.Facebook.com/OwningAnAllotment.

For a full color version of this book please download the Kindle version to your tablet, e-reader or computer. This is a free download from Amazon for anyone who has purchased the print copy of this book.

If you have enjoyed this book, please leave a review on Amazon

TABLE OF CONTENTS

INTRODUCTION

Pumpkins are one of the most fun vegetables to grow. The plants can grow to a massive size and the fruits themselves can become massive. Pumpkins are a much more popular vegetable in the United States than in the rest of the world and is, without doubt, one of the most understated and underused vegetables there is. They are not for everyone though because of the space requirements but there are still some varieties you can grow in small spaces.

However, this book isn't growing small pumpkins, it's about growing big pumpkins; pumpkins so big you can't lift them! In fact, it's about growing pumpkins so big you have to hire a tractor to move them!

Growing giant pumpkins takes time and effort but it is thoroughly rewarding, and it is certainly something people will want to talk about! I remember the first year I grew a large pumpkin on my allotment and everyone was talking about it, wanting to see it and, most importantly, wanting to know just how much it weighed! After that first year it became an unspoken competition to see who could grow the biggest pumpkins!

Growing giant pumpkins is more than just putting a seed in the ground, it is about a number of factors, all of which you will learn about in this book, including:

- Selecting the right seeds
- Germinating your seeds
- Planting your pumpkins in the right conditions
- Feeding them properly
- Caring for them and protecting them against pests
- Harvesting at the right time

All of these contribute to a giant pumpkin and if you ignore any of these you can end up with a pumpkin that hasn't reached its full potential. Don't worry though, we will go through all of these steps and more in this book, teaching you everything you need to know to grow giant pumpkins at home.

You may now be thinking that growing giant pumpkins is just a bit too complex but let me tell you that you can make it as easy or as complex as you want. Even if you don't give your pumpkins all the attention they need you can still grow one over a hundred pounds easily. Give them a bit of love and you are pushing two hundred pounds and more!

At the time of writing the world record for the largest pumpkin is held by a Swiss farmer, Beni Meier, whose record breaking pumpkin weighed in at 2,096.6 pounds! That is a phenomenal weight, as heavy as a small car and he transported the pumpkin using a specially made vehicle!

It is unlikely you will grow one this size in your first year, but once you start applying what you learn in this book you are going to be well on to growing your own giant pumpkins, winning local and regional competitions and hopefully moving on to national competitions too!

The giant pumpkins can be used for cooking and you can make tons of pies and soup out of them (I have a freezer full of pumpkin puree and soup which lasts until pumpkin season comes round again). However, they can be a little bit watery and bland compared to the smaller varieties which often have a much fuller flavor. As you are likely to save many of the seeds you often do not have as many to roast so a lot of people will grow giant pumpkins for fun and then smaller varieties for baking and carving. Larger ones can have extremely thick flesh, often two or three inches thick, meaning they are not good for carving and certainly they cannot be carried out at Hallowe'en.

Growing giant pumpkins takes some work and dedication and in this book you will learn everything you need to know to grow your own giant pumpkins. This is a fun hobby and you can make some really delicious meals with your giant pumpkins, which is as good as normal pumpkins for eating … more on those towards the end of the book, including my favorite pumpkin pie recipe, which has to be tried!

Enjoy growing your own pumpkins and having fun watching them grow and beating your own record every year as you grow these fun fruits that are fun to grow and delicious to eat too!

CHOOSING A SEED VARIETY

Seed selection is probably the most important choice you are going to make in growing a giant pumpkin. With the right seed you are laying the foundation for success. There are a multitude of pumpkin varieties, which will be discussed in the next chapter but realistically only a few of these are giant varieties. The majority of pumpkin varieties are designed to produce jack-o-lantern sized pumpkins which are good for cooking, easy to handle, transport and sell.

There are a number of pumpkin seed varieties you can buy off the shelf that are going to grow into a good sized pumpkin. What you will do from these is save the seeds from the largest year upon year until you get to the super giant sized pumpkins. This is how many of the gardeners grow such big pumpkins, but if you are looking for a pumpkin between 100 and 400 pounds then there are some packets of seeds easily available and affordable.

One of the most popular varieties is the Atlantic Giant, which can be found in many garden stores or you can buy them online from Amazon. However, when you are buying online make sure you get them from a reputable supplier as often you can find people selling poor quality seeds with a low germination rate. Read the reviews of sellers or look to a reputable online garden retailer who will have these seeds in stock. Atlantic Giant is easy to get hold of, are affordable and has a high germination rate.

If you want to grow seriously big pumpkins then you can get hold of specialized seeds from giant pumpkins. These are much harder to get hold of and you are going to be charged a premium price for them. You will either need to contact a giant pumpkin grower or you will need to find a specialist supplier.

Often you can find major seed companies selling the seeds from prize winning pumpkins. You can easily pay $20-$25 or more for just two seeds, but they come from pumpkins weighing in at well over 1000lbs if not close to 2000lbs!

This is by far your best way of getting giant pumpkin seeds but you are going to be paying a premium for the seeds and you need to be very careful to ensure you get the seeds to germinate.

Genetics plays a massive part in growing giant pumpkins which is why championship growers horde their seeds so carefully and they are so expensive to buy. When you buy seeds from a pumpkin of this size you are much more likely to get a pumpkin of a similar size or bigger because it is genetically predisposed to producing a pumpkin of that size. If you can afford it I would recommend buying these pumpkin seeds as it is a short cut to growing giant pumpkins and you will not have to go through several years of saving seeds until you get to pumpkins of that size.

There will be local suppliers in your country or area who can sell you similar seeds, you will just have to search around and find them.

Do not skimp on buying the seeds and certainly do not buy a small variety of pumpkin and think you can grow it into a giant pumpkin, it will not happen. Giant pumpkins are going to come from giant pumpkin seeds so get the right seed and you will be well on your way to success!

PUMPKIN VARIETIES

There are a lot of different pumpkin varieties, and they do not always grow into giant pumpkins. However, just for completeness and so you know all about the different varieties, here is a list of all the different types of pumpkin on the market at the time of writing together with a little bit of information about each one.

Aladdin – A large jack-o-lantern type of pumpkin that is resistant to powdery mildew

American Tonda – deeply ribbed pumpkins where the outer part of the rib is dark green and the inner part turns from orange to yellow. Stores well and looks fantastic

Amish Pie – they don't grow too big but are great for cooking and store well

Atlantic Giant – a giant variety of pumpkin that is favored with growers and will produce pumpkins up to 400 or 500 pounds in weight easily plus its good for cooking too though perhaps not as full in flavour as the smaller varieties

Baby Bear – a small pumpkin that is ideal as a pumpkin bowl or for kids to carve

Baby Boo – another small pumpkin that is white in color though will turn yellow in the sun. They don't store particularly well but they are great for kids to carve

Baby Pam Sugar Pie – a great baking pumpkin with a thin skin and sweet, fine grained flesh

Big Rock – a medium sized pumpkin that is a dark orange color and is great for jack-o-lanterns

Big Max – a large pumpkin, able to grow over 100 pounds with a bright orange shell. Whilst they can be used for baking they can be watery and stringy, not having as much flavor as smaller varieties

Charisma – another medium sized pumpkin with some powdery mildew resistance

Cinderella – named due to their resemblance to the pumpkin used for Cinderella's carriage, these are great looking pumpkins that taste good, being a French heirloom variety

Cotton Candy – a variety with a whiter skin colour that is quite resistant to insect damage plus is great for carving

Fairytale – another French variety that is deeply ribbed, turning a deep mahogany color when ripe. This is a great in pies

Full Moon – a large pumpkin, growing over 100 pounds but considered quite bland and watery for cooking

Hoolidan – very small pumpkins that are a light gold color and make for superb soup bowls

Howden – a deep orange variety that has thick walls and strong handles, making them great for carving, though they do suffer from powdery milder

Howden Biggie – the same as the previous variety but larger and great for carving

Iron Man – a small bright orange pumpkin that has a hard shell and strong handle, great for kids as they are hard to break!

Jack-be-little – another small pumpkin that is great for kids, being so small they will fit in the palm of your hand and last for months if kept out of direct sun

Jack-be-quick – similar to the previous variety but a bit bigger and stores well

Jarrahdale – an Australian native variety that is quite hard to get hold of, but great for baking and decorating

Kakai – orange with dark green ribs this is a tricky pumpkin to grow but the seeds are hull-less and fantastic roasted

La Estrella – orange / green in color with fruits between five and ten pounds these are usually grown as an ornamental variety

Lil' Pumpkemon – mini pumpkins that are edible with cream and orange colors

Long Island Cheese – a heirloom variety with a flat shape and sweet flesh, able to be stored for up to a year out of direct sunlight

Lumina – a ghostly white pumpkin with a deep orange interior that is great for cooking and carving

Marina Di Chioggia – an Italian heirloom variety that is a deep blue / green in color which is also great for cooking

Neon – an early maturing pumpkin that are orange throughout their life though they don't store well or grow very big

New England Pie – a traditional heirloom variety from the East Coast of the USA which weigh in at a few pounds but are good for baking

Old Zebs – very similar to Neon though it has weaker handles and tends to an orange color very early on

One Too Many – a moderately sized pumpkin that is a cream color with orange speckles and stripes though it can be a bit inconsistent in size and crop

Pic-A-Pie – a reasonable sized pumpkin that crops well and is great in pies

Prizewinner – one of the giant pumpkin varieties with a dark orange skin and a very definite pumpkin shape to it

Queensland Blue – an Australian variety with deep ribbing though it stores well and is great for baking

Rock Star – a medium to large, though not giant, variety with a dark orange color

Valenciano – a great pumpkin to decorate and for baking with a light colored flesh which makes for unusual pies. Be aware it can sometimes be stringy and watery so may need to be pureed and reduced before baking

Wee-Be-Little – a small pumpkin that is great for kids and carving, usually slightly larger than a tennis ball and rounded in shape

SUCCESSFULLY GERMINATING YOUR SEEDS

Once you have your seeds you need to plant them and get them to germinate successfully. If you have bought seeds from a giant pumpkin then you are likely to have paid a premium and will want to ensure you get a very high germination rate.

In order for the seeds to germinate you need:

- Viable Seeds – good quality seeds that are solid, i.e. not hollow and are recent; old seeds have a poor germination rate
- Soil – a good quality seed mixture that is light, free draining and sterile
- Water – your soil needs to be kept moist but not soaking wet
- Heat – seeds need heat to germinate and a temperature of 80-85F will help to ensure a high germination rate

When to plant pumpkins depends on your growing season. Typically you will start them off about three to four weeks before the last frost which in most temperate areas you are starting towards the end of April, early May, though in colder climates this could be later and in warmer climates it will be earlier.

You can plant pumpkin plants directly into the soil outside but if you are growing giant pumpkins then you need as early a start as you can get so you start them off indoors, giving you a head start on the growing season.

You need some pots to grow the seeds on. Don't start your seeds off in a tray because you will have to transplant them and this will harm your pumpkins. They do not like being moved or handled and transplanting them can run the risk of killing them or stunting their growth.

You want a small pot about four or five inches across, though you can use peat pots if you want. These will biodegrade in the soil and the roots will push through them though I personally have found they dry out very quickly and this can damage your seedling and make it hard for the roots to grow through. A pot like the one pictured is just fine. You will need one pot per seed. You will not be planting more than one seed in a pot as you do not want to disturb any of your pumpkin plants at any stage if you can help it.

Whatever pots you choose they need to have suitable drainage holes in the bottom otherwise the soil will get too wet and the seeds will end up rotting.

Fill the pots with a good quality potting compost, one that is free draining is best. You can mix some horticultural sand in with the compost and some vermiculite if you want to give the seeds the best start in life. A good quality compost will feed the seedlings for the first week or two and help ensure they thrive. Using a seed starter compost will work well for you though you can mix up your own if you prefer.

Next you put the seeds in the compost on their sides. You can carefully and lightly file the edges of the seed using some fine sandpaper or a nail file as this will help them germinate by letting the moisture get into the seeds. This isn't so important with smaller varieties of pumpkins but with giant varieties it can help the leaves emerge as the shells are very thick. The picture here shows some pots with seeds near the top ready to be pushed down and covered with compost.

Some people will put their seeds in the freezer for a day or two to help them germinate by simulating the winter freeze. In reality this doesn't seem to make a big difference and whilst some people like to do it, there is no evidence it helps improve the germination rate.

As pumpkin seeds are so hard it will help them to germinate if you soak them in warm water (not hot) for between two and six hours. This helps to soften the shell which will help the leaves emerge and encourage germination. Germination is triggered by moisture getting into the seed and this process will help encourage germination. Some people will soak the seeds for 24 hours but there isn't enough difference in success rate between the two timings to make it worth soaking the seeds for longer. If you do soak them for longer you run the risk of the seeds going moldy because they are too wet.

The seeds then need to be covered with about an inch to an inch and a half of compost. Do not plant them any deeper because the seedling may have problems emerging from the soil if you do.

Water the pot thoroughly so the soil is moist, but not wet; the state you want to keep it in whilst it is germinating.

The seed will germinate in between seven to ten days and if your seed hasn't sprouted after ten days then sow some more as they are unlikely to germinate.

Heating the pots from the bottom will help the seeds to germinate. You can use a germination mat if you want to, which will speed up the germination time. Once the seedling has sprouted you need to remove the germination mat as otherwise you run the risk of damaging the roots.

Most people will put their pumpkins either in a greenhouse or on a sunny windowsill. One of my techniques to help keep them warm and germinate is to create a mini greenhouse around each pot using plastic wrap. This is a very quick way to keep your seeds warm and help them to germinate rapidly though you need to keep a close eye on them as in the wrong conditions the seed scan rot. I tend to leave the plastic wrap a little loose so that there is some air circulation and then remove it once the seedling pushes through the soil. You will typically see your seed germinate in about a week or slightly less with this method.

If you prefer you can use a seed propagator for your pumpkin seeds though you need to keep a close eye on them and remove them when they have started to grow to avoid damage to the roots.

Check your pumpkin seeds daily because if any problems do appear you need to take action sooner rather than later to try to save your plants. Do not keep moving your pumpkin seeds or poking around in the pot; let nature do her job and you'll get your pumpkin seedlings soon enough.

The baby pumpkin plants will be kept indoors for about four weeks, by which time they will be large enough to be planted outside. Water them regularly, to ensure that they are moist but not wet and feed them after the first couple of weeds with a diluted liquid fertilizer. Be careful not to get the leaves wet when watering, particularly if they are on a sunny windowsill as it can cause leaf burn which could kill your seedlings.

You will not plant your pumpkins out until the danger of frost has passed because they are very susceptible to damage by frost due to their hollow stalks and high water content. If there is any chance of frost when they have been planted out then cover them with a cloche or horticultural fleece to keep them warm so they survive.

DAMPING OFF DISEASE

This is a common diseases found when you start your pumpkins off indoors and is where you get a white mold on top of the soil. This thrives when it is cold and wet with bright light. It will quickly spread over the soil and then damage your seedling. It does happen occasionally when you grow your plants on the windowsill or use the mini greenhouse method detailed above.

The easiest way to prevent this is to ensure that the conditions for your seedlings are ideal for pumpkins, i.e. warm, free draining and not too damp. If you do find this mold on your seedlings then you need to place the plant in direct sunlight straight away. Stop watering your seedling and allow it to dry out, ideally you want to water from the bottom using a saucer and tip away excess water. This will allow the plant to suck up the water it needs rather than the water sit on the top of soil.

Scrape as much mold as you can off the soil and then stir the top quarter inch of the soil, to help it dry out. Do this a couple of times a day. Make sure your plants are somewhere with good air circulation as this will help them to dry out.

LOOKING AFTER YOUR SEEDLING

After a week to ten days you will see your pumpkins start to poke their head above the soil and this is when you can breathe a big sigh of relief and know that you have completed the first step, but the journey has just become as your seedlings need care and attention before they are planted out and make their own way in the world.

Pumpkin seedlings need light, and lots of it. You want direct sunlight, i.e. put them on your windowsill but make sure you do not get water on their leaves or that their leaves touch the window. The former will cause leaf burn and the latter can cause the leaves to wilt and be damaged by the temperature differential. You will need to turn the seedlings as they will have a tendency to leave towards the light.

Depending on how far north you are, this might not be enough for your pumpkins and you may need to supplement the light with some grow lights. The seedlings should be between six and eight inches below the lights; remember that you will need to move the lights up as your plants grow.

Pumpkins are thirsty plants but do not overwater them as it is one of the main causes of dead or damaged seedlings. Once every couple of days will be plenty, making sure your plants dry out between waterings.

For the first week or two in the pot your plants should have plenty of food if you have used a decent quality potting compost. After about a week though, water your plant with a diluted liquid fertilizer to give it a bit of a boost.

Your seedlings are ready to plant out after about four weeks and you may start to see the roots poking out of the bottom of the pot. We'll talk more in the next chapter about planting out your seedlings. Ideally you do not want to transplant your seedlings to another pot as it will upset your pumpkins and can stunt their growth or even kill them. If you do have to transplant them then warm the soil first and be very, very careful!

PLANTING OUT YOUR PUMPKIN PLANTS

After the fraught time with your seedlings you are then ready to plant them out. By now you should have some strong seedlings which should have at least two leaves, though usually they will have more. They may start to lean rather than growing straight up, which is okay, just make sure that the seedlings do not get tangled together as you can damage your seedlings when you are separating them.

Before you put them in the ground you need to select the site, prepare the soil and more …

Site Selection

Choosing the right site to grow your pumpkins is very important because the soil and climate conditions are vital if you want to grow giant pumpkins.

As with many other vegetables, pumpkins like lots of sun and will grow best in full sun. This way you are maximizing their ability to produce energy from their leaves through photosynthesis which will help to produce the biggest possible fruits. The other advantage of full sun is it helps to keep the leaves, fruits and stalks dry as they will dry earlier in the day which will minimize the chance of diseases such as powdery mildew developing.

The really fussy growers claim that even the direction you grow the plant in is important and that you should grow it from east to west to maximize sun exposure, but this doesn't make much of a difference, if any. Other people will tell you that you have to grow your pumpkins on a downward incline on a south facing slope. This is all well and good but not everyone will have access to this type of site to grow their pumpkins and you have to make do with what you have. A southern exposure will give your pumpkins more sunlight, particularly towards the end of summer when the days are shorter and your pumpkins need the extra sun to ripen.

However, don't worry if you haven't got these conditions, you can still grow giant pumpkins in normal conditions; these are just the ideal conditions which are the absolute best for pumpkins.

Pumpkins are very thirsty beasts and so like soil that has a high water table as the roots will dig into the soil and drink plenty. This extra water will help your pumpkins grow really big! If you do not have a high water table then dig in plenty of organic matter to make the soil retain water better, though you do not want a clay soil as that will retain too much water which can cause problems. However, if you prepare the soil properly, which will be discussed shortly, this doesn't matter.

Wherever you decide to site your pumpkins you need to be aware of the principles of crop rotation which means you do not grow pumpkins in the same area two years in a row. If you do then this allows pests to build up in the soil and the soil itself will become depleted of essential vitamins. By rotating your crops you are minimizing this problem. In an ideal world you rotate your crops over a three year cycle though in reality this may not be possible so at the very least do not plant your pumpkins (or any gourd/squash) in the same area two years in a row.

Find somewhere suitable to grow your pumpkins and remember that the vines can grow twenty, thirty, forty feet or more in length, though you can manage the length of your vines as you will find out later in this book. Just be sure that the plants are not going to grow on to your lawn, under trees or somewhere else where you don't want them to grow when you are picking the site.

PREPARING THE BED

If you are serious about growing a giant pumpkin then this step is very, very important as it is the secret to growing really big pumpkins. If you don't do this then you are going to find you struggle to get a truly giant pumpkin.

Wherever you are going to plant a pumpkin you need to dig out a hole about five feet wide and about three feet deep; yes, it is a lot of work but it is worth it. Fill this hole with manure and compost and mound it up so it stands about a foot above the normal soil level. You can throw in kitchen scraps and other waste material that will break down into compost. Press this down but do not compact it as the more compact the soil the harder it will be for the roots to spread.

If you are using kitchen scraps then you need to make sure this is done leaving enough time for it to break down otherwise it will harm your plants. Typically you want to perform this step a month or two before planting so that the compost is broken down and ready for your plants. If you use well-rotted manure and compost then you can do this a week or two before planting. Typically I would do this step in March though this will vary according to how far north you are.

This is the best way I've found for preparing the soil:

- Put a layer about three or four inches of compost in the bottom of the hole, including stuff that hasn't decomposed fully
- Put a layer of straw in the hole, about an inch deep
- Add some leaf mulch or grass mulch
- Add three or four inches of manure

Repeat this layering until you have filled the hole and then mound it up so you can plant your pumpkin seedling in the middle of the mound. Remember, push these layers down and compact them a little, but not too much as you need it to be easy for the roots to get through the soil but firm enough to support the plant.

You can add fertilizer to this mix if you want though the mix itself has plenty of nutrients. I will sometimes add pelleted chicken manure to the mix for some extra feed.

Every giant pumpkin grower will have their own "secret sauce" that they use to make their pumpkins grow. One of the best secret ingredients I have found are worm castings which are a nutrient dense fertilizer that really gives plants a boost. You can learn all about how to produce your own worm castings at home, which is easier than you may think, in my book on worm farming here.

If your soil is heavy clay or very sandy then you will want to amend the soil for an area of around twenty feet around the central mound in order to really give your pumpkin the best conditions. Admittedly this is a lot of work but if you do this soil amendment then you will see even better results.

MOUNDING THE BED

We touched on this earlier on and it is important that you mound up the central point in your bed where you are going to plant your pumpkins. You can mound this up to between six and twelve inches as it will help your pumpkins a lot.

This mound helps to improve drainage and prevents the build-up of bacteria as well as the drowning up the roots. With the soil raised up like this it helps to heat the soil around the seedling which is particularly important on the earlier, cooler spring days.

THE REST OF THE BED

Pumpkins send out vines for many feet in every direction and these make a big difference in whether or not you get a big pumpkin or a BIIIIIIIIIIIIG pumpkin! You see, these vines can put down secondary roots which will pull up more nutrients which will make your pumpkins grow even bigger!

Therefore it is very important that you condition the soil outside of just the initial planting area. You cannot predict where these secondary roots will form, so conditioning the whole area means that your pumpkins have access to the nutrition they need to grow to a giant size.

This soil needs to have a neutral pH and be rich in manure. You can dig in well-rotted manure and compost into this soil and be very, very generous about it! You literally cannot dig in enough of this to this area as it is vital to producing giant pumpkins. Admittedly you are unlikely to dig in as much as you can around the seedling area, but you should dig in as much as you can. Just ensure that whatever you put in the ground is suitably decomposed so that there is no risk of burning or damaging your pumpkin plant.

GROWING IN THE SUBURBS

A single giant pumpkin plant is more than capable of covering several hundred square feet by the time you are ready to harvest which to the suburban garden could well be a problem! However, you do not need to have to dig up all your lawn but towards the end of the season you may well lose some of the lawn but the grass will usually survive under the pumpkin.

However, you can prune your pumpkin and keep it under control and you will end up with a very big pumpkin, even a monster compared to those you can buy in the store but not a giant.

If you have limited space then plant your pumpkin at the edge of your garden so that the vines can spread outwards along your yard. Cut the lawn around the vines so it does not compete as much with the pumpkin plant for nutrients, though be very careful not to damage your vines.

Your vine will grow out across your lawn and where the vines grow place about three or four inches of compost and train your vine, using stakes if necessary, along this line of compost. Your vine will grow secondary roots along this compost line which will help feed your pumpkin and make it grow really, really big!

Don't worry about your lawn as the grass will continue to grow under the compost and it will not damage it too badly. At the end of the growing season you can pull the vine up, rake in the compost, cut your lawn and sprinkle some fresh grass seed over the lawn and you will have a lawn that looks as good as new when spring comes.

HARDENING OFF

Your pumpkin seedlings will have become used to being indoors so taking them outside into real weather where it is cooler and they are exposed to the elements is going to be a huge shock for them. Transferring your seedlings straight in the ground from the windowsill will cause a lot of shock to the plant which can stunt its growth or even in the worst cases kill the plant. This transplant shock is a serious issue for seedlings so it is vital you follow these instructions to harden your plants off.

Hardening off plants is a process some of you will be familiar with. It's basically where you expose a plant grown indoors to the elements gradually over time to help it become accustomed to the different climate conditions. Hardening off is performed over a period of a week or two which gives the seedling plenty of time to adjust.

Take your pumpkin seedlings outside and put them in a warm sunny spot for a few hours. Make sure you wait until the spot has warmed up and then bring them inside before the temperature starts to drop again. For the first few days do not put them out if it is raining or windy as this could cause damage to them.

If you look closely at your seedlings you will see that they are become stockier, which means they are stronger and better able to survive the wind and weather outdoors.

Every day, let the plants sit outside for longer so that they experience greater temperature differences and different types of weather. However, if there is any risk of extreme weather or frost bring your seedlings back indoors immediately as this could kill them.

When it gets close to the time to plant them out or you are after the last frost date for your area you can let your plants stay out overnight, so long as it doesn't get too cold. This is going to help the plants get used to the cooler night time temperatures for when they are planted out.

It can be very useful to own a cold frame for hardening off your pumpkins. This allows your plants to stay outside for longer with protection from extremes of temperature. You want one with covers that you can life up during the day when it is warmer and then at night you put it back on. These can be made of glass, polycarbonate or plastic and can vary from $20 to $30 up to $300 to $400 for the most expensive ones. You can see more about cold frames on Amazon. If you want to save some money then buy one at the end of the growing season ready for next year as garden stores will be shifting their summer stock for Christmas stock and have them discounted.

TRANSPLANTING YOUR SEEDLINGS

Now is the moment of truth when you are going to take your plants and put them outside. However, before you do I would recommend buying a cloche for each plant and a roll of horticultural fleece just to be on the safe side. Whilst you plant out after the last frost date, there can still be a risk of frost and having these to hand means you can protect your delicate plants should a surprise frost happen.

Your pumpkin plants need between 50 and 100 square feet per hill when you are planting them, with giant pumpkins needing more space purely for the size of the fruit. At a minimum you need to allow between six and eight feet between mounds and space in rows around 15 to 20 feet apart.

When transplanting you need to be very careful to avoid transplant shock which can stunt or slow the growth of your plants and in the worst cases kill them. Transplant shock is caused by a number of factors including:

- Damaged or Disturbed Roots – it is very easy to damage the tiny feeder roots which can slow the growth of your plant whilst it regrows them. You need to be very careful not to damage any roots which is one reason some growers use peat pots but if you handle the plants with care you are not going to cause any damage
- Cold Temperatures – this is why you have to harden off your seedlings to prepare them for the great outdoors as well as be prepared with protective equipment should a surprise frost appear
- Dry or Soggy Soils – your seedlings want moist soil but if the spring rains have left a soggy soil then you want to wait for it to dry out a bit first. This is why the pumpkin grower will typically prepare the soil and mound it up, as discussed previously
- Hot Sunlight – direct sunlight can cause your seedlings to wilt, particularly if you have damaged their roots during transplanting. Many growers will erect a shade over their seedlings for the first few days whilst their seedlings get used to the bright light and establish their root system. If you have hardened off your plants then this shouldn't be so much of a problem unless the roots have been

damaged

The best type of day to plant out your seedlings is a cool day with plenty of cloud cover. If the day is too windy and too bright then it can wilt the seedlings or damage them, even if you have hardened them off. Provide shade for a few days if the sun isn't going away!

At the top of the mound where you are going to plant your pumpkins dig a hole that is around twice the size of the roots. If you are using peat pots then just put the pot in the hole and the roots will grow out through the pot walls and the pot itself will decompose.

For plastic pots, make sure the soil is dry and then place your hand palm down on the pot so that the stem is between your forefinger and your middle finger. The picture shows you how (though this is me repotting a tomato plant rather than pumpkin the technique is the same). You then turn the plant upside down and tap the bottom of the pot a couple of times. The plant should slide out of the pot and you are left holding an upside down plant!

Some people will loosen the roots from the root ball at this point which is valid if the plant has become pot bound but with a seedling I would recommend leaving it alone so that you avoid the risk of damaging the roots. The more you fiddle with the roots, the more chance of you causing some damage.

Place the pot-less seedling into the hole you dog and then back fill with the soil you took out, which should be a mixture of soil and compost. You can mix in some peat moss if you want for some extra drainage.

Press down firmly, but not too hard, around the base of your seedling, carefully avoiding damaging the leaves or roots.

Once this is done, you need to water it in at the base of the plants, avoiding getting water on the leaves as this could damage your seedling. Some people will fertilize their seedling when they transplant it but if you have prepared the soil properly then you will not need to.

Over the next few days keep the soil moist but not soggy or wet to give the seedling chance to put out a good root system. You may not see your seedling grow for a few days or even a couple of weeks and start worrying that something has gone wrong, but don't worry. After transplanting the seedling concentrates on establishing a root system and then when this in place you will suddenly see your seedling grow and then it will continue to grow in epic proportions every day!

POLLINATING YOUR PUMPKINS

The bees and insects will typically do an excellent job of pollinating your pumpkins and if you plant some bee attracting flowers near your pumpkins then you can ensure that you get these helpful insects to pay you a visit. However, in some cases there may not be a large number of bees in your area or you may want to pollinate particular flowers on your pumpkin plants.

If you are aiming to grow a giant, prize winning pumpkin, only growing one or two pumpkin plants or there are other members of the squash family growing nearby then hand pollination is a great idea to ensure your plant produces pumpkins. With other squashes growing nearby you run the risk of cross pollination so rather than produce a giant pumpkin you get some hybrid instead.

Your pumpkin will start to produce flowers usually in July with the male flowers appearing first. It can be a week or two before the female flowers appear so don't worry, be patient and keep tending to your pumpkin plant as it will produce those flowers you need.

Male flowers are very easy to spot as they have a straight, thin stem that is several inches

long. The stamen in the middle of the flower contains the pollen and it should not be used until it is mature, i.e. it easily comes off the stamen on to your finger. Typically you will find there are several male flowers for each female flower on your vines. When a female matures you will see at least one mature male flower ready for action. The picture here shows a male flower forming, you can see beneath the flower there is no baby fruit and just a straight stem. It is very easy to tell the difference between the male and female flowers.

Female flowers have a tiny baby pumpkin located between the flower and the vine. The female flower is much closer to the vine than the male flower. In the

picture here you can see a pollinated female flower that is closing and dying, leaving the baby pumpkin behind on the stem. Notice how the stem between the pumpkin and the vine is much shorter than on the male. This stem will become the handle on a jack-o-lantern.

Female flowers also have a more complex stigma in the middle of the flower which is multi-segmented. The male flower has a single stamen in the middle of the flower. The difference between the flowers is very obvious though the fruit behind the flower really gives it away. In order to pollinate your pumpkin you need to take the pollen from the male flower and apply it to the female stigma.

You can tell if pollination is happening naturally because when the female flower dies and drops off the baby pumpkin will start to grow. This is known as fruit set. If there was no pollination then the baby pumpkin will shrivel up and die.

In order for full pollination the male pollen needs to get to all segments of the female flower, which a bee does perfectly. If it doesn't then there is a chance the pumpkin will not grow to its full potential.

If you are using pesticides or a farmer in your area is using pesticides then you can find the local insect levels are lower than normal, meaning there are not as many natural pollinators at hand. By planting bee attracting flowers that flower early to mid-July near your pumpkins you can gauge the local insect levels and determine if you need to take over and manually pollinate or whether you can let nature get on with it. Of course if you want to select which fruits grow then you will want to hand pollinate anyway.

If you are aiming to grow giant pumpkins then every day that the pumpkin is not growing counts so you will want to take a hand and pollinate the pumpkins yourself. You certainly do not want to run the risk of none of your flowers being pollinated and missing the growing season completely.

Hand pollination is actually quite easy though you will need a steady hand. Find a female flower that is open and choose a male flower. This is best done early in the morning as the female flowers will close up later on in the day.

Touch the stamen of the male flower gently and see if any pollen comes off on your finger – you should see tiny yellow specks if it does. Pull the petals off the male flower carefully so you don't shake off all the pollen so that the stamen at the middle is exposed.

You can then either remove the stamen and rub it on the stigma, use a cotton bud or your finger. My personal preference is to remove the stamen, using scissors to cut it to avoid shaking loose all the pollen, and then touch the stamen to all parts of the stigma. I then leave the stamen in the female flower just to be absolutely sure.

You will want to pollinate a number of fruit on each of your pumpkin vines and then you can choose which ones you want to keep and which to discard. The best fruit will usually come from female flowers with five or six sections to the stigma. You can increase the chances of pollination by covering the hand pollinated female flower with a fine screen such as a nylon stocking to ensure nothing else interferes.

Once pollination takes place what is called fruit set occurs, which is where the female flower dies off and the baby pumpkin starts to swell. A number of factors can influence this, not least of which is your fertilization program. When your plant is first growing it needs a fertilizer high in nitrogen which will promote leaf, vine and root growth. However, too much nitrogen can delay flowers forming so when you want the plant to produce flowers you need to reduce the amount of nitrogen fertilizer you are using and use one that is higher in phosphorus, which promotes flowering and fruiting.

Some other factors can influence fruit set, including an early summer heat wave which will cause plant stress and can cause the baby fruits to abort. An early heatwave can also stop bees from doing their job, meaning hand pollination becomes essential. If the weather is very hot and your fruit are dying off then don't worry and keep looking after your plant as when the weather cools again new female flowers will appear and your pumpkins can be pollinated.

If you know other people growing giant pumpkins then you can always cross pollinate with them in order to widen the gene pool available to your pumpkins. Swapping male stamen with them is a great way to give your pumpkins a bit more of a chance and if you are saving the seeds ensure that you don't breed out desirable qualities from your pumpkins.

PROTECTING THE FRUIT

As your pumpkins mature you will want to protect them and keep an eye on them. Firstly you need to protect them from the sun as this will harden the skin, reduce the growth and also increase the risk of it splitting. If you notice your pumpkins will stay hidden under the leaves and only come out towards the end of the growing season as the leaves die back. This is when they are exposed to the sun, harden and turn an orange color, eventually splitting to release their seeds.

Stretch a tarp over posts above your pumpkin which will stop the rain and sun getting to it. If you don't want to risk damaging your pumpkins by putting in posts then you can drape a white sheet over your pumpkin instead.

When your pumpkin starts to grow you do not want it sitting on the bare soil as this could lead to rot if the soil gets too wet and can encourage pests to attack your pumpkin as they come up from the soil.

You need to lift your pumpkin off the ground to protect it and this needs to be done whilst they are small as leaving it to when they are bigger could result in damaging the pumpkin or the vine, if you can even move it!

Straw can be placed under your pumpkin though this is not ideal as it will rot and can attract rodents who will use it as a bed.

A better way is to place a wooden pallet or large square of wood under your pumpkin, but remember, do it when it is small so that you don't damage your pumpkin. These will keep the pumpkin off the soil and reduce the risk of rot due to the pumpkin sitting on wet soil as well as help prevent soil borne pests from getting up to your pumpkin. Landscape fabric or a piece of plywood with sand on it (to stop the wood damaging the pumpkin) works really well. This is also going to help keep the rodents off your pumpkins but you will still have to patrol for the pesky slugs and snails … more on them later on! Whatever you put under your pumpkin, make sure that water cannot pool on it as this will rot your pumpkin. It needs to be able to drain so your pumpkin can sit on something dry.

CHOOSING WHICH FRUITS TO KEEP

Once the flowers are successfully pollinated you will see the flower wilt, die and eventually fall off. The tiny pumpkin will visibly increase in size though it will appear to grow slowly initially. After a few days you will see it increase in size noticeably as every day it is bigger and bigger.

Some people will recommend that you place the pumpkin in an upright position to help it grow round and smooth on all sides. This is practical for smaller varieties of pumpkins but for giant varieties it just doesn't work. Do this too early and you end up with a squat shaped pumpkin and do it too late then you can damage the secondary root system and the vines. Having lost pumpkins due to fiddling like this my recommendation is that you leave them alone once you have lifted them out of direct contact with the soil. The risk of damaging the vine and plant far outweighs any benefits from positioning your fruit.

However, with giant pumpkins you do need to position the fruit on the vine, which is something to do before it gets too large. This will stop the pumpkin from pulling itself off the vine as it grows and if you don't do it then you can end up with stress, kinks and tears in the vine or the stem of your pumpkin. This reduces the flow of nutrients and water. In the worst cases the stem will actually split off from the vine, which is the umbilical cord for your pumpkin. Even the smallest bit of damage can reduce the size your pumpkins will reach.

For giant pumpkins you want to position the vine that is near the fruit so it is loose and it can move upwards as the fruit grows without causing any damage. This does mean that you should not encourage any secondary root systems to form near to the fruits so you have this free movement in the vine. Unless you intervene there can the chance of stress and damage to the pumpkin as it goes over two hundred pounds.

Left to its own devices the pumpkin vine will produce a dozen or more fruits but because you want to produce giant pumpkins you need to limit each vine to one or two fruits. Any more than this and the vine will be spreading its resources across a dozen or so fruits to produce good sized pumpkins instead of concentrating its resources in a few fruits to produce giants.

When choosing which pumpkins to keep you want a fruit that has a stem which is perpendicular to the vine. This lets the pumpkin grow away from the vine rather than on to the vine where it will squash it. The perfect position is where the fruit is growing at a ninety degree angle to the main vine which then turns away from the fruit after the junction point. If the vine does not naturally do this then you can use a stake to train the vine away from the fruit so there is plenty of space for it to grow into a giant.

If the pumpkin is not in the ideal position then move it into the right position over a period of a few days a little at a time. Moving it too much can cause damage to the vine.

For about three feet on either side of the pumpkin make sure no secondary roots form because if they do these will put stress on the vine and cause tearing as the pumpkin grows to a giant size.

Unfortunately if the vine does tear there is very little you can do about it. If you do find a tear in the vine then you can cover it with soil and in most cases it will produce secondary roots and it should recover.

Giant pumpkin growers will remove all but one fruit from the vine, even go as far as removing any additional male / female flowers before they form so that the pumpkin vine can focus its energy on the one single pumpkin. If you only have a couple of plants in the ground you may want to leave two pumpkins on the vines so that you have an insurance policy and get more than one pumpkin. However, for seriously giant pumpkins you will remove all but one fruit.

If you keep more than one fruit on the vine you can still grow big pumpkins, but they are unlikely to be giants. I've had a 118lb. 82lb and about half a dozen 10-15lb pumpkins off a single vine before (which I will admit I didn't care for as much as I should have done). So even leaving all the fruits on the vines you can still produce some good sized pumpkins that will get people talking.

For giant ones though you will care much better for your plants and just have a single fruit on the plant. For competition growing this is absolutely essential and ideally you will have multiple vines so that you have a backup in case a plant gets damaged.

The question is though, which pumpkin do you keep? With up to a dozen fruits on the vine it can be a big decision, particularly if you are entering a competition with your pumpkins. My advice for choosing which pumpkin to keep is as follows:

- The really giant pumpkins are grown on the main vine, but this does not preclude success on secondary vines. Ideally you want to keep a pumpkin that is on this main vine but if other criteria are met you may want to consider one on a secondary vine
- You need to measure your pumpkins daily to determine which fruit is growing the fastest and then you keep that one, removing the rest. It may be the first pumpkin to set grows the quickest or it could be the third but without daily

records you will not know

- If shape is important then look for one that is round. A pumpkin that is slightly long but still round is a good shape to keep as it will fill out when it grows. However, if it is long then it can turn an oval shape but then most giant pumpkins are peculiar shapes and only smaller varieties are the perfect pumpkin shape
- Look at the stem joining the pumpkin to the vine as a long, fat stem is better. Longer stems will stress less as the pumpkin grows and fat stems mean more nutrients can get to the fruit to help it grow

At the start of July (or just after pollination) choose two or three pumpkins on the main vine that are about ten feet or so from the planting site. About three weeks later, around the 20th July you will choose the fastest growing pumpkin and remove the rest. This pumpkin is then positioned perpendicular to the vine and something is placed underneath it – sand will work as will wood, pallets or anything that allows the air to circulate and keeps the fruit off the soil. You also need to train the rest of the vine, using stakes if necessary, to grow away from the pumpkin so it has plenty of space. At this stage you may also want to erect a tarp on poles over the site of the pumpkin so you are not trying to drive poles in the ground when the plant is much bigger.

Check your vines every couple of days and if any new pumpkins appear they need to be removed. If any roots appear on the main vines within three to four feet of the pumpkin these need to be removed too. You can support the vines leading to the pumpkin stem with something soft like Styrofoam to help reduce any stress to the vine.

The set pumpkins have to be at a good angle of around ninety degrees to the vine in order for them to grow into a giant size. If they are not at this angle then as the pumpkin grows it will cover the vine which will restrict the flow of nutrients and even kill the plant. It can be easier to move the vine rather than the pumpkin but whichever you are moving, do it slowly and over a period of about a week as you can easily damage the vine or pull the pumpkin off! There will be no warning if a pumpkin is about to come off the vine so just take it easy and don't rush. You need to do this when the pumpkin is about the size of a basketball or a bit smaller. Any bigger than this and the risk of causing damage increases significantly.

From experience I've found that the pumpkins which are round and tall tend to grow into the largest pumpkins. Pumpkins on the main vine are closer to the main source of nutrients so tend to grow larger, even when you grow secondary roots. Remember, choose the pumpkin that is growing the fastest and has the best shape.

As the pumpkin grows so the vine is going to lift up in the air with the pumpkin. If it is not positioned correctly it can pull itself off the vine and pick itself! As the pumpkin grows you need to support the vine around the pumpkin so that it isn't sagging as it can snap under its own weight. Make sure no side vines grow around the pumpkin as they can cause damage so train them away from the pumpkin. A leaf will typically be growing at the junction with the vine and the stem and this should be removed with a sharp knife or scissors (carefully) as it can scratch and damage your pumpkin. If necessary, remove any secondary vines that are getting in the way.

Remember that you need to protect your pumpkin from direct sunlight to protect it from premature aging. Blue or orange tarps are the best according to most growers, though avoid black as it will concentrate the heat too much which could damage the pumpkin. Between two and four weeks before harvest time remove this tarp so that the sun can give the pumpkin its distinctive orange color and harden up the skin, which is essential for when it comes to moving it!

Once the vine has grown about ten or twelve feet beyond the set fruit you can cut the end of the vine off and bury it under the ground. Secondary vines will typically be cut off and buried between eight and twelve feet long. These are also buried in the ground. Doing this will stop the pumpkin plant putting its energy in the vines and instead make it focus its attention on the fruits so they grow huge.

If you are aiming for giant pumpkins then this stage is absolutely vital. If you just want big pumpkins or a good crop of pumpkins then it is not so important to pick the fruits off, but you still need to terminate the vines so that the fruits on the vine swell and ripen.

Pruning the Vine

We talked briefly in the previous chapter about terminating the vine so now I want to go into a bit more detail about how you prune and care for your pumpkin plant. The main vine it its life blood and if it is damaged then it can kill your plant or stunt your pumpkins. However, the vine is very easy to damage and is surprisingly fragile so if you want to produce mammoth pumpkins, then this is how you care for the vines!

Runners and Side Shoots

You are going to find these all the way down the main vine and secondary vines are to be encouraged, though they require managing. These need to be trained away from the main vine, typically in a Christmas tree pattern with the main vine being the trunk of the tree and the secondary vines coming off at an angle of between 45 and 90 degrees. You can alter the position of the vines using carefully positioned stakes and train them to grow away from the fruit so they are not cut off and damaged as the pumpkins grow.

When you are training the secondary vines out you need to ensure they do not cross over each other as you need to have access to the plant without running the risk of stepping on a vine and causing damage.

You will find tertiary vines growing off your secondary vines with pumpkins; they are prolific growers. If you see any of these tertiary vines they need to be pruned off straight away so that your pumpkin focuses its energy on the pumpkins, not on green growth.

Secondary Roots

These are very important when it comes to growing giant pumpkins as they help the plant get more nutrients into its system which can then be used for the pumpkins. They are, without question, the secret of the giant pumpkin growers and will make the difference between a large pumpkin and an enormous one!

Secondary roots will develop on the vine at the base of each of the leaf stems. This is something you need to encourage as much as you can because it also helps to anchor the plant to the ground and prevent wind damage. Remember, do not encourage any secondary roots within about four feet of a pumpkin because the vine needs to be able to move as the pumpkin grows.

If you do not encourage your pumpkin to grow secondary roots then you are going to struggle to get a truly monstrous pumpkin. These not only help to anchor the vines to the ground, protecting them from wind damage, but also feed the plant and fruit. In the worst case where a break, tear or kink occurs in the main fine, secondary roots can actually keep the pumpkin plant alive and the fruits growing.

It is very important that you promote the growth of these secondary roots, but remember, not within about four feet of a fruit! Promoting secondary root growth is really simple, you just cover an area of the vine with some soil! Most growers will cover the junctions between the main and the secondary vines with soil as well as bury the ends of the vines in the soil. This will create some secondary roots though you can cover any point on the vine. How many secondary roots you encourage is up to you, but a lot of growers will encourage A LOT of these roots as it means more nutrients for the fruit!

After covering some of the vine with soil you just keep watering those areas and it won't be long before you have secondary roots appearing. If you want to really encourage your pumpkins to grow then instead of using soil to cover the vines use a good quality compost. Because it is high in nutrients it will help the vine grow even stronger and give it a much needed boost.

These need to be fertilized just like the main root. Personally I find it very difficult to work out where all the root points are as it can be hard to find them in all the leaves and vines, particularly as you need to be careful not to damage your plant. I either push bamboo canes into the ground to mark the spot so I know where to water (as you never water on the leaves of a pumpkin) or I push plastic tubing in to the ground (three or four inches in diameter is best) so that I can pour water down the tubing which then goes directly to the roots of the plant. This helps me remember where I have to water so that the water goes directly to the roots and isn't wasted on the rest of the soil where it will encourage weed growth.

Pruning Vines
Pruning vines is essential because otherwise your vines will take over your garden and much of the energy of the plant will go into growth rather than into pumpkin development.

The main vines are usually pruned somewhere between ten and fifteen feet after the last fruit whilst secondary vines are pruned at around ten to twelve feet from the main vine. A single pumpkin plant can have two or three main vines and each main vine is capable of producing a giant pumpkin. Whilst pumpkins can be produced on secondary vines these are less likely to grow to the giant proportions you are after.

Trimming the vines is pretty easy, just cut the end from the vine and then put a shovel of two of soil over the cut end. It isn't essential to bury the vine end but it helps by reducing moisture loss and the risk of disease. Use a good quality, sharp pair of secateurs to make the cut as you do not want to risk tearing the vine which could potentially introduce disease.

Remember after pruning your vines you want to ensure the secondary vines are at an angle of between 45 and 90 degrees from the main vine so that the vines do not grow over each other or into the pumpkins.

Usually when you prune the vine you will see a lot more new vines growing to take their place. Some will be secondary vines, others will be tertiary vines. Once you have done the initial pruning you can pinch off these extra vines so that they do not consume vital energy from your plants. Changing your fertilizer mix to one that has a bit less nitrogen in and more phosphorus and potassium will help the plant focus on fruit growth rather than leaf growth.

You can get away without trimming your plants but realistically you need to cut the ends off at the very least because otherwise they will grow, and grow, and grow, meaning energy that should have gone into produce a big pumpkin went into extending the vine instead. However if you are planning on growing a giant pumpkin then pruning is vital as you need every drop of energy possible to go into the pumpkin. Trimming the vine also means that the plant puts its energy into ripening fruit which means at the end of the season all of your pumpkins are ripe rather than just a few.

KEEPING YOUR PUMPKIN PATCH WEED FREE

As you want your pumpkins to grow as big as possible it is very important that you remove all competition for resources from your pumpkin patch. Watering and feeding at the roots of the plant will help to reduce the weeds, but they are still going to grow.

Whilst your plant is a seedling you need to hoe the patch regularly and keep the weeds under control. Preventing them from getting established means that the nutrients you have dug into the soil will not be wasted on weeds but instead will go to your pumpkin as it grows. Once the pumpkin is larger a smaller hand hoe can be used (wear gloves though as pumpkins are prickly) to remove weeds and avoid damaging the pumpkin vine.

As the pumpkin grows bigger so its large leaves will crowd out the weeds, but they hardy and will still grow under the leaves, though not in as large a quantity. Regularly check under the leaves and remove any weeds before they have a chance to get established.

Avoid the use of pesticides or weed killer on your pumpkin patch as it is likely to affect your pumpkin and probably kill it. In the best cases your pumpkin will be absorb the chemicals which you will then ingest if you eat the pumpkin. Weeding by hand is the safest and best way to remove the weeds from your pumpkin patch without causing any harm to your giant pumpkins.

FEEDING & WATERING YOUR PUMPKINS

Pumpkins are very greed plants and they thrive in rich soil, which is why so much effort goes into preparing the site. This will pay off big time as your pumpkins start to put down their roots and suck up all the nutrients you have given them. However, whilst we have gone into a great amount of detail about preparing the site for your pumpkins we now need to talk about how you feed your pumpkins as they are growing.

Finding the right feeding formula for your pumpkins is down to trial and error, depending on the soil conditions, type of soil, how you prepared the pumpkin patch, the pH levels, how much rainfall you get and so on. You do need to be careful in your trial and error because applying the wrong type of fertilizers in the wrong quantities can actually harm your plants and in the worst cases even kill them.

FERTILIZER CHEMISTRY

You need to have an understanding of the chemistry behind fertilizers in order to understand properly how to use them and what your plants need. When you buy fertilizer it will have an NPK ratio displayed somewhere on the packaging which is three numbers, e.g. 5-10-5.

This gives you the ratio of the main components of the fertilizer, e.g. 5-10-5 would give you the ration of Nitrogen (N), Phosphorous (P) and Potassium (K) displaying the percentage of each element in the fertilizer. Depending on where your pumpkin is in its lifecycle will depend on the ratio required.

Nitrogen

Nitrogen is the fuel for leaf, root and vine growth and is fertilizers high in nitrogen are applied early in the growth of your plants. High nitrogen levels means plenty of lovely green leaves but it is also very harmful to your plants and should never be applied directly to the vines or leaves as it can burn them.

However, too much nitrogen and it will slow down or reduce the fruits and flowers appearing on your vine. If you have a huge vine with loads of giant leaves on but not flowers, stop using a high nitrogen fertilizer for a week or two and your plant will direct its energies to creating fruit and flowers rather than leaves. Large amounts of nitrogen can also cause wilting on your plants.

Phosphorous

As your vine moves towards fruiting and flowering you will switch to a fertilizer that is higher in phosphorous such as a 5-10-5 or 5-15-5 fertilizer. If you are not entirely sure which fertilizer to use then stick with one of these two ratios and it will be a good all-rounder.

Phosphorous does not burn your plants and does not dissolve as well in water so giving your plant too much phosphorous isn't going to cause it a great deal of harm.

Potassium

This element promotes healthy fruit growth and once the fruit has set you should either switch to a fertilizer higher in potassium or feed your pumpkins with extra potassium. This will not burn your plants but giving your pumpkins too much potassium can cause them to grow too rapidly and they end up splitting their skin. Therefore take it easy early on so that you do not cause any damage to your fruits.

Minerals and Micro-Nutrients

As well as these major elements there are numerous trace elements that will hopefully be in your soil if you have prepared it properly. These contribute to plant growth and are important to the health of your pumpkins. Most fertilizers will contain varying levels of micro-nutrients and if you vary the fertilizers you are using then you will get a broad spectrum of these essential elements.

Liquid Fertilizers

Liquid fertilizers are a fantastic way of getting nutrients directly to your plants. These can be applied as a foliar spray (direct to the leaves) or applied to the main or secondary roots. If you are growing giant pumpkins then this is going to be your best friend and you will want to apply liquid fertilizer with every watering. Pumpkins are very greedy plants and literally cannot get enough food. For a giant pumpkin you need massive amounts of food so it can support a pumpkin of the size you want

Liquid fertilizers do tend to be a bit more expensive than other fertilizers but apart from that there are no downsides as they are easily absorbed by your plants. You can make your own easily with nettle tea, comfrey tea, worm tea or compost tea all being popular home-made fertilizers which are perfect for your plants.

Perhaps the only issue with liquid fertilizers is that it can be hard to find one other than the standard 5-10-5 ratio. As it is water soluble it needs applying more often, which is why most people apply it every time they feed. If you are going to be away from your plants for a few days then apply a solid fertilizer like pelleted chicken manure which will break down over a few days.

Whilst liquid fertilizer is fantastic it is not a substitute for compost and manure which should be dug into your soil every season. This is why it is so important to prepare the soil properly with plenty of nutrition because then when you add the liquid fertilizer you avoid this issue.

Fish and Seaweed Fertilizers

Anyone who grows giant pumpkins will sing the praises of fish and seaweed fertilizers as they usually come in a liquid form and, whilst low in N-P-K, they are loaded with micro-nutrients and are organic. These are excellent for both foliar and root feeding and should be used often. It is also thought to help prevent plant disease just like taking vitamin supplements helps to keep you healthy.

If you are growing giant pumpkins then regularly doses of fish and seaweed fertilizers should be used in addition to your regular feeding schedule to give your plants that little extra help.

Foliar Feeding

This is a very simple yet important process for feeding your plants where they absorb the food through their leaves. All you do is dilute a liquid fertilizer according to the manufacturer's instructions and then spray the leaves and vines. Once or twice a week is enough, more often and you run the risk of damaging your leaves, but it will help your plants have healthier leaves, which means photosynthesis will work better and your pumpkins grow larger.

Start foliar feeding early in the growing season and you will have healthier, stronger plants and much larger fruit.

FERTILIZING STRATEGY

So, now you have a good idea of the chemistry of fertilizers you need to plan out a strategy for applying them. This is a rough plan that you can use though it will need adjusting according to your area, the climate and your personal experiences. One of the keys for growing giant pumpkins is to experiment with different feeding regimes to determine what works best where you are.

- Prepare the bed with a good mix of compost, manure and other nutrients – usually done around February so that it can break down before you put the pumpkins in the ground
- Before your transplant your seedlings mix in a general purpose fertilizer to the soil where you are going to place the seedlings
- Foliar feed your pumpkins once or twice a week
- Apply dry fertilizer once every two weeks (pelleted chicken manure is great)
- Apply liquid fertilizer every time you water your pumpkins but apply it directly to the roots
- Until the flowers appear use a fertilizer that has a high amount of nitrogen
- When the flowers appear use a fertilizer that has a high amount of phosphorous
- Once the fruit has set move to a high potassium fertilizer

Whenever you are using a fertilizer always make sure you read the directions and apply as per the manufacturer's instructions otherwise you run the risk of damaging your plants.

If you are new to growing pumpkins and want to make things easier then just use a well balanced fertilizer such as a 5-10-5 ratio which is applied every two weeks and watered in. The liquid fertilizer is applied as a foliar feed once or twice a week. If you are busy or if you are new to growing giant pumpkins this can be an easy way to get started without adding in extra any extra complexity.

Every giant pumpkin grower will have their "secret sauce" for growing giant pumpkins whether it is worm castings, liquid fertilizer or their own mix. These are usually closely guarded secrets and few are going to share but with time, experimentation and keeping good records you will work out your own feeding regime.

One myth with giant pumpkins is to feed them with milk, which frankly does not work. All you end up with is a pumpkin patch that stinks and no real benefit plus it can attract predators. However, adding some molasses to your watering can does seem to make a difference as the sugar in the molasses does benefit your plants.

WATERING YOUR PUMPKINS

Pumpkins are very thirsty plants, just think about how much water goes into the fruit plus the vine itself is very watery too. Whilst water is very important for your pumpkins, too much is detrimental to its health, particularly if the soil gets too wet. If you have prepared your soil properly then it should retain enough moisture but be free draining enough.

If the soil becomes too wet then it will rob oxygen from the soil and dilute nutrients, which is harmful to your plant. The soil should not be allowed to dry out so the ideal conditions are a moist soil rather than a soaking wet one. You may hear people telling you to let the soil dry out so that the plant grows a stronger root system, which to a degree is true, but with giant pumpkins this will reduce the size of your fruits as the plant concentrates on growing its root system instead.

For giant pumpkins though they can grow anywhere from 40 to 50 pounds in a single day (yes, I am serious) so providing your pumpkins with less than optimum conditions for even a day can have an impact on the final weight!

Pumpkins are very thirsty plants and so you need to water them often. The best place to grow pumpkins is somewhere with a high water table, but the rest of us, it means watering by hand, and often. If you are not growing giant pumpkins and just want big pumpkins then you can get away with less frequent watering but your pumpkins won't reach their full potential.

For most of us, we need to choose a sunny position and then water either by hand, through irrigation or by hose. As summer approaches so you need to water your pumpkin more often, though please ensure you do not get water on the leaves. Getting water on the leaves can cause powdery mildew which will kill your plant, usually before the pumpkins full ripen. This is one of the biggest mistakes people make with pumpkins or in fact any squashes.

My personal method is to mark the root areas of the pumpkins either with bamboo canes or plastic pipes and then water directly to the roots. I have lost pumpkins from watering on the leaves before and it is soul destroying to see your hard work rotting away. If you are watering by hand then splashing water on the leaves in the morning is forgivable as the leaves will dry out but in the evening time the water will not evaporate and your plant is more likely to become diseased.

By far the best way to water your pumpkins is either through an underground soaker hose or a drip line, though understandably these systems are not practical in all locations. This can continuously drip water to the root system which means you have a lot less work to do hauling water. It also minimizes water going on the soil and getting to the weeds.

Using an underground soaker hose does require a bit more work on your part preparing the soil. You can position your hoses underground as concentric circles and then turn on each ring as the plant expands, which means water will get to all parts of the plant, including the secondary root systems. Alternatively you can plan which way your pumpkin will grow, lay the hoses and then try to train the pumpkin to grow along the hose.

Another option is to just bury the soaker hose under the mound where the main vine will be. This is usually okay and will water the main root ball and then you can water the secondary roots by hand.

An even easy way of laying a soaker hose is to lay it on top of the soil with the holes pointing down and then shove some soil over the top of it. This is simple and quick and allows you to lay the hose as the vine goes.

Watering cans are another very important tool for the giant pumpkin grower. With a soaker hose and a watering can you can look after your pumpkins and give them all the water they need.

The watering can is used to sprinkle water directly where you want it to go, e.g. to the main root area or secondary root areas. It allows you to target your watering so you are not just soaking the soil and giving the weeds water. The only disadvantage of this is that it takes time but it does let you keep an eye on your plant and check it for any problems.

Above ground sprinklers are really not recommended with pumpkins. Whilst they are great at watering large areas and watering them well, the water is not directed and goes everywhere. This means the weeds are watered but worst still, the water gets on the leaves which is just a recipe for disaster, particularly on warm, muggy summer nights. If you have to use an above ground sprinkler then do so in the morning only which should give the leaves time to dry off. Ensure that your sprinkler delivers a soft spray as pumpkin leaves are quite delicate and can be damaged by a strong stream of water.

A garden hose is a common way to water pumpkins in the sub-urban garden and has the same risks as an above ground sprinkler. It does take more time to water and many people will get bored and end up not giving their pumpkins enough to drink. The other downside is that the flow of water can be stronger which could end up with damaged leaves.

Irrigation ditches are great because the water does not get near the leaves but the downside is it uses a lot of water and the water gets to everything, not just the pumpkin. For the home gardener and irrigation ditch just isn't practical, being more common in commercial growing situations.

Pumpkins need a lot of water and you should look at giving your pumpkins between 15 and 20 gallons of water every three or four days. As pumpkins do most of their growing at night it is beneficial to give them a good water in the evening, but ensure it is directly to the roots. On hotter days they can also benefit from a good drink in the morning to help them cope with the heat.

If you are watering by hand then give your pumpkin either a good soaking until the water puddles on the surface of the soil. Whilst the pumpkins need up to twenty gallons every few days, they often benefit from watering daily to help protect them from the effects of the heat.

Harvesting & Storing Your Pumpkins

The end of the growing season has come and you now have giant pumpkins on the vine. Now you need to know how to correctly harvest and store them so that they will last for several months and you can use them for cooking or display them. How you move your giant pumpkin … well that's an issue you'll have to overcome but just ensure you are very careful! I moved mine one year through a combination of a wheelbarrow and car but it took a long time to shift it!

You must not pick your pumpkin before it is ripe because if you do it will not store as well as it could do, meaning it is more likely to rot and go off before you have a chance to use it. Remember though that when you pick your pumpkin you need to cure it which will help to prolong its life.

Pumpkins are ripe when they have a uniform color over the whole skin. The part that was face down on the soil may well be a different color but the rest of it should be more or less one color. The skin is going to be firm and when you press it with your thumbnail it should not dent.

Pumpkins must be harvested before a hard frost. A light frost will just kill the vine and the fruit should be fine but a hard frost will damage the pumpkin so the fruits have to be harvested and moved inside before the frosts set in.

Harvest time is when most accidents happen with pumpkins such as they get dropped, bumped, bruised, scratched and so on, all of which are an open invitation to rot and pests. Make sure you are very careful handling your pumpkin and moving it, particularly if it is big! Not least you need to be careful you don't damage yourself trying to life a giant pumpkin.

The fruit needs to be cut from the vine with a sharp pair of secateurs, leaving a handle that is around three or four inches long. The handle is attractive, though check particular competition rules for handle requirements, but it also means the fruit is less likely to rot whilst in storage. Whatever you do though, do not try to carry a pumpkin of any size by this handle as the stem usually cannot support the weight of the pumpkin and will break off.

Before you store your pumpkins, check them for any bugs and insects which need to be removed before they go into storage. If there is any mud on the pumpkins then clean it off with a damp cloth (dry the area afterwards) before you store the fruit.

Pumpkins need curing after harvesting, which usually means putting them in a shed or leaving them out in the sun, depending on the weather conditions. The ideal conditions are a temperature of between 80 and 85F (27-29C) and a relative humidity of between 80% and 85%. They will need to cure for about ten days which will help to harden the skin as well as heal and scratches or cuts.

Once the pumpkins are cured they need storing in a cool, dry location with good ventilation. The temperature should be between 50-55F or 10-13C. Do not store pumpkins near any other fruit that is ripening such as pears or apples as these will give off ethylene gas which is going to shorten the storage life of your pumpkins. Ensure your pumpkins do not touch each other in storage as that will encourage rotting and they need good air circulation so lift them up off the floor if you can on wooden pallets. Whatever you do, do not heap your pumpkins in a pile as this will generate heat which is going to rot some pumpkins.

Always regularly check your pumpkins, probably at least once a week and then either use or dispose of any fruit that is damaged or decaying.

With good storage and ideal conditions pumpkins will last for two or three months, though some varieties will last longer. I tend to store mine and then roast and puree it so I can freeze it or make it into a dish and then freeze it for later in the year.

Giant pumpkins are stored in the same way as smaller pumpkins but obviously with their size they are harder to store because you cannot get them into a shed easily. You can usually get them into a garage but you will need help moving it. Most giant pumpkins are consumed shortly after showing with the seeds kept and sold or replanted and the flesh used to make pie or soup.

WEIGHING AND MEASURING YOUR PUMPKINS

If you are serious about growing giant pumpkins then you will be measuring your pumpkins almost daily and keeping track of its growth, helping you to understand what is influencing its growth. You will want a cloth tape measure, a notebook and a pencil to keep track of the growth. Weighing your pumpkin whilst it is on the vine is not a good idea because it involves moving it which could either damage it or cause it to detach from the main vine.

Tracking the growth of your pumpkin helps you understand how it is growing. You will understand how much it grows every day which can help you with your fertilizing and watering schedule. Taking this regular measurements is going to help you estimate the weight and track your progress towards a monster pumpkin!

There are ways of estimating the weight of the pumpkin from these measurements based on people's growth of giant pumpkins. It involves a bit of mathematics but if you search online for "giant pumpkin weight estimation tables" you will find the authors of that work and their estimation tables.

If you are not estimating the weight then you still need to track the size of your pumpkin and keep a diary of how you have fed and watered the plant. If you are growing multiple plants and trying different methods of feeding and watering then this will help you understand exactly what works and what does not.

You will want to take two measurements of your pumpkins. Firstly you will measure the circumference at the widest point and then you will take a similar measurement over the top past the stem. However, do not try to move the pumpkin or anything whilst measuring it as you run the risk of doing some damage so if you cannot take both measurements don't worry about it. As an estimate you can measure half way round the pumpkin and then double it, assuming the pumpkin is an even size. This won't be 100% accurate but it will be close enough for your purposes.

Once you pick the pumpkin you will need to weight it. Smaller pumpkins can be weighed on bathroom scales which will often go up to a couple of hundred pounds, though it can be tricky to position the pumpkin on the scales so you can read the display.

For giant pumpkins you will have to take it somewhere to get it weighed, which could cost you some money for transporting it. However you transport it, you will have to move it carefully to avoid damage. If you are entering your pumpkin in a competition then you need to move it to the competition site where it will be weighed. Look at the competition rules and see what they expect from your pumpkin with respect to the handle length, how it needs to be transported, what it needs to rest on and so on. Moving giant pumpkins is not easy and for the larger ones you may need a crane, flatbed truck or a tractor!

If you are serious about producing giant pumpkins then you need to keep track of the size which will help you understand how it is growing. Track the weather conditions, the amount of rain, your feeding schedule and so on so that you know what influences the growth of your pumpkins. By tracking what you do with your pumpkins you can determine what works in producing giant pumpkins.

Entering Your Pumpkins into Competitions

Many people who grow giant pumpkins will want to enter them into competitions and there are bound to be competitions in your area. You will have to search around online or ask people who grow giant pumpkins where the competitions take places. Many towns have their own vegetable competitions that you can enter your pumpkin in and various county shows have the same competitions.

The rules for judging will vary from competition to competition so you need to get hold of the rules before you start growing so that you can ensure you meet their criteria and can enter your pumpkin into the competition.

Typically rules will look something like this:

- Pumpkins must be grown, cared for and entered by the contestant
- Contestants may enter a single pumpkin per household or family
- Pumpkins weighed at other contests are not eligible
- The pumpkin much be either 100% or a combination of the colors red, yellow, salmon and orange
- The pumpkin must be free from rot, holes, cracks, chemical residue and serious soft spots plus be in sound and healthy condition
- The vine (handle) should be one inch long

There will be other rules but they tend to be standard ones like the judge's decision is final, detailing the prize money and so on.

Growing giant pumpkins for competitions is good fun though for a lot of people just the satisfaction of growing a giant pumpkin is enough.

PROTECTING YOUR PUMPKINS FROM PESTS

Pests are one of the biggest problems for the giant pumpkin grower, particular when the plants are young and starting out. At this stage they are very tasty and very delicate, so every pest in the neighborhood will try to eat your baby pumpkins. Even when they grow bigger and the skins harden so the slugs and snails will still try to chew them, sometimes managing to burrow through the skin into the inside.

Keeping pests off of your pumpkins is going to be a lot of work as fencing and netting keeps out the larger pests whilst smaller pests need to be removed by hand or with carefully selected repellent sprays.

Large Pests

Deer can be a problem for some growers as they will feed on the tips of the vines and new leaves. Later in the year they will enjoy the ripe pumpkins. If you live in an area with deer then you will need fencing to keep them off your pumpkin patch.

Rabbits are another potential problem and are fond of new leaves and young fruits. These again have to be kept off by netting and fencing. If you are going to build a fence then you need to bury wire mesh about two feet down into the ground to stop rabbits getting under the fence and into your pumpkin patch. In the worst cases you may have to resort to hunting and trapping to keep the rabbit population under control.

Mice and moles can be a huge problem as moles will dig under the ground and disturb the roots whilst mice will gnaw their way through the fruits. Using poison is not recommended as it will get into the soil and therefore into your food. Traps and deterrents are the best way to keep these out of your pumpkin patch. If you build a good wooden fence around your patch and then use fine wire mesh around the bottom three feet (and buried two feet down into the ground) this should keep most of these pests at bay.

Squirrels and chipmunks can be a real pest as they love pumpkin seeds and will raid your patch at harvest time, gnawing through the skin to get to the seeds. Hot pepper sprays will keep these away from your fruit but you need to spray daily and in particular after ever rain. Putting a plastic mesh over your pumpkin patch so it meets with the fence will keep them out but it is a lot of work and expense. Traps and hunting will help to keep them under control.

Woodchucks are another problem in some areas and will climb over or dig their way under fences. They are also able to chew through pretty much anything except metal and so are extremely difficult to keep out. Hunting and trapping are really the only ways to keep these pests under control.

If you are hunting and trapping any of these pests then you need to be aware of any local laws and obey them otherwise you can find yourself in legal trouble.

Insects and Bugs

Bugs are going to be a big problem for anyone growing pumpkins and there are plenty of insects looking forward to you planting your pumpkins so they can feast on them. Practicing crop rotation will help to keep pest populations down to a minimum but there is still the risk of the pests finding your plants.

Aphids will suck the sap on your young plants and cause the leaves to curl. They will typically be found on new growth and can be picked off by hand and crushed between your fingertips. You may want to wear gloves here, though not everyone does. Regularly check your pumpkins, particularly where there is new growth and remove any aphids – I check daily as aphids can stunt the growth of your plants. In the worst cases you may have to resort to insecticides but get an organic one that is safe to use on food crops rather than one laden with harmful chemicals.

Melon thrips are another potential pest and they attack the leaves, flowers and fruit. These can be a major problem but good hygiene will keep them under control and regular checks help to stop them getting established. If necessary you can use an insecticide to kill these off.

Cutworms can affect young seedlings and again kept under control by good crop hygiene and the careful use of insecticides.

The pumpkin beetle can be a problem and you will notice it by the leaves having shot holes in them. You are likely to experience fruit drop and this can be treated with insecticides. If you practice good hygiene in your growing area then this is not likely to be a problem.

The cucumber beetle is one of the most common enemies for any vine crop and can damage the leaves as well as transmit diseases. This beetle isn't found in every area and crop rotation will help to keep it under control. Sprays can be used if necessary, particularly in mid-season when they are abundant.

Occasionally you will see deformed fruit and stunted growth in the vine which is down to the Rutherglen bug. This is another one best treated with insecticides.

Providing you practice good crop hygiene and look after your plants properly you are going to reduce the risk of any of these insects getting to your pumpkins. Rotating your crops on a three or four year cycle will also prevent the build-up of pests in the soil which will danger of pests damaging your precious crop.

There are lots of different insects out there and most are completely harmless to your pumpkins and are even beneficial. Some will even eat the insects which are harmful to your crop. This is why you need to be very careful with pesticides because you end up killing of all the insects, not just the harmful ones. Organic gardening methods are by far the best because you are not ingesting the chemicals you use when you eat the food you grow. Minimizing the amount of chemicals is only a good thing, particular with the concern many people have for the environment.

Unfortunately, for giant pumpkin growers, some sprays are likely to be necessary as you cannot risk pests damaging your pumpkin or plant and holding back its growth. If you can, use organic sprays where possible but if you keep the soil free from leaf debris, water at the base of the plant and practice good hygiene in the area where you are growing pumpkins then you will minimize the risk of insects. Many more can be removed by hand and if you check your plants daily then you can catch a problem before it becomes serious.

Slugs and Snails

These are likely to be your biggest problem and they will eat the baby seedlings and then the baby fruit plus they will cause damage to the rind of grown pumpkins, eating holes and causing a great deal of damage.

There are lots of tales about how to control them from egg shells to coffee grinds to sand but none of them are effective. They may prevent some of these slimy pests getting to your pumpkins but it won't stop them all. You can use slug pellets but you do have to be careful with these as they are toxic to children and pets but they are effective yet will still only kill some of these critters.

When growing your pumpkins you cannot rely on a single method of slug and snail control because your plants are going to get eaten. Don't think that just because your pumpkins are big they are safe from pests, you need to be even more vigilant because many giant pumpkin competitions will disqualify any fruits with damage on them. Slugs and snails can still chew threw the skin of a fully grown pumpkin, though it will take them a bit of time!

Anyone who tells you that slugs and snails don't bother pumpkins obviously has never grown one. You need to protect your plants and you need to do it right from the start. Here's my strategy for keeping these pests off of my crops.

- Clear the area including the surround six to eight feet of ANYTHING that a slug or snail could hide under. This means remove pots, leaf debris and anything else that could harbour these pests. Whilst you are doing this, destroy any slugs or snails you find.
- As you are digging the soil, break up any lumps as these pests will hide under these. If you see any slugs, snails or their eggs (small white balls clustered together) then remove and destroy them.
- When you plant your seedlings ensure there are no weeds on your pumpkin patch. The bare soil will discourage slugs and snails from venturing out into the opening.
- Surround each seedling with a ring of coarse horticultural grade sand – do not use any other sand as it can contain chemicals which will kill your seedlings. This ring needs to be about six to eight inches wide and an inch or two thick. It will need regular topping up, particular after rain.

- Place two beer traps near to each pumpkin seedling. Take a plastic soda bottle (about three inches in diameter) and cut the top off. Sink it into the ground so the neck is about half an inch above the soil then half fill it with beer. This will need emptying every couple of days.
- Every evening at dusk go out and search your pumpkin patch for slugs and snails, looking under leaves and everywhere you can. Take a torch if you need to. Remove and destroy any pests you find.

One thing you can do is plant some lettuces away from your pumpkin patch as these can attract the slugs and snails and keep them away from your pumpkins.

With this strategy you are going to keep slugs and snails away from your pumpkins but it is a lot of work. However, if you are planning on growing a giant pumpkin because if your seedlings are killed you can grow more but you will miss out on two or three weeks growing time which could make the difference in your pumpkin winning.

Vine Borers

These are another potential problem for pumpkin growers that can be very serious. The larvae will dig its way into the vines near the base, eating away at the vine and sucking out the juices. They then get into the vine and move up the vine, virtually invisible to you until the damage is irreversible. You will typically notice these pests when you see the pumpkins suddenly stop growing as quickly and after this the vine will shrivel and start to die.

You can cut out the infected area of vine and if you have secondary roots then your plant is likely to survive, though the pumpkin may not achieve its full potential. When you cut the vine, treat it with appropriate sprays and then bury the two ends to promote secondary roots. This isn't a common infestation, but it does happen so you need to be aware of it and keep an eye out for it.

Squash Bugs

These are sucking insects that will attach themselves to the stems and leaves of your pumpkin plants. They can be controlled through a spray such as Sevin. They are actually quite hard to control because they hide underneath the leaves, meaning you have to lift every leave and spray the underside. Smaller bugs are easier to control than larger ones so it is something you need to keep an eye out for if these bugs are a problem in your area and take action the moment you see them.

These bugs are most commonly found either just after your transplant the seedlings or as the flowers start to form. You are unlikely to get large infestations of squash bugs during a single growing season they can build up in the soil if they survive the winter. This is another good reason for you to rotate your crops; it prevents the build-up of bugs like these.

Applying a pyrethroid insecticide will keep these bugs under control, and it should be applied the moment you notice the bugs on your plants. If you don't take action then these bugs will multiply and stronger insecticides will be required.

Insects and other pests are a very real problem for the pumpkin grower but you can find that you have few problems other than slugs and snails most years. However, if you are growing giant pumpkins you need to be extra vigilant because any lost growing time can mean your pumpkin doesn't reach its full size. Damage to your pumpkin can result in it being disqualified from competition so keep a close eye on your plants and protect them from pests so you can grow a giant pumpkin!

DISEASES THAT AFFECT PUMPKINS

We've talked about some of the pests that affect pumpkins but there are also a number of diseases. Again, these aren't going to be common but there is a chance your plants could get one of these diseases so you need to keep an eye on your plant and take the appropriate action at the first sign of problems.

However, good hygiene in your pumpkin patch, watering at the base of the plant, regular feeding and crop rotation will help reduce the risk of diseases and hopefully you won't have any issues with your pumpkin plants.

Black Rot

This is a fungal disease also called gummy stem blight and is a very serious disease, though usually you won't see it until you store your pumpkins. If you notice black lesions on your fruit before harvest then likely it has this problem and when you store it the fruit will collapse.

This disease originates in the pumpkin patch and so you need to ensure you are using disease free seeds, practice a two or three year crop rotation plan and use fungicide sprays if required.

Anthracnose

This is an occasional problem with pumpkins and is also a fungal disease most common in conditions of high humidity and warm temperatures. Usually this disease will show itself when the fruit is in storage, which usually means it won't make it to the competition. This fungus overwinters in debris so keeping your site clear of debris and rotating your crop on a two or three year cycle will keep this disease at bay.

Powdery Mildew

Probably the most common problem found on pumpkins and you will see the leaves are covered with white powder which is the fungus. This develops then the leaves get wet and then don't dry out fully, usually from evening watering of a pumpkin and getting the water on the leaves. On the warm summers night the fungus develops and once it does, it is very hard to get rid of.

Water at the base of your plant and ensure you do not splash water on the leaves as this will help to significantly reduce the risk of this problem. Destroy and do not compost any infected plant material and rotate your crops. You can use fungicides on your pumpkins when you see powdery mildew which will, in some cases, keep the disease under control.

Bacterial Wilt

This will be seen through the leaves wilting and browning. In some instances you will see the leaves firming up again at the end of the day only to get worse the next day. This disease is often confused with a lack of watering or the temperatures being too high. If you are watering your pumpkins and it is still wilting then you can cut a leaf about an inch from the vine. If the sap is yellow in color and stringy then you have bacterial wilt.

Unfortunately there is no cure for this disease and you should remove the infected plant and destroy it immediately. Do not compost it.

Prevention Better Than a Cure

With all of these diseases, prevention is far better than a cure. Crop rotation ensures that diseases cannot build up in the soil and will significantly reduce the risk of disease. Good hygiene and watering at the base of the plant will ensure that the conditions of your pumpkin patch are as hostile as possible to diseases.

After harvesting the fruit some people will leave their pumpkins in the sun to cure. This is good but you need to ensure that the fruits do not get wet because it will encourage the development of disease. The last thing you want is to grow a world record breaking pumpkin only to find it develops a disease in storage and cannot be exhibited.

Any pumpkins that have rot or any blemishes need to be removed and destroyed, the same goes for any leaves that look infected. Always use a sharp pair of secateurs to make any cuts so as to reduce the risk of introducing any infection.

Whilst some people suggest you should water your pumpkins in the evening, this is only going to work if you are using an underground soaker hose. Using a watering can is a recipe for disaster as it is far too easy to splash water on the leaves, which is then going to cause disease. Water in the morning or during the day. If you have to water in the evening, which many of us do, then be extremely careful to get the water to the base of the plant only.

Some giant pumpkin growers will take a very precautionary approach and spray their pumpkin plants with fungicide and pesticides just to be on the safe side. This can work and if you are growing for competitions you cannot risk your plants getting infested. However, if you are planning on eating your pumpkins or you don't plan on showing them then you can avoid the use of chemicals as it is better for you and the environment.

Diseases are not a common problem, with the exception of powdery mildew, but they can occur. Keep a close eye on your plants and check them regularly, usually as you water, to ensure there is no infections. Any diseased plant material should be removed and destroyed immediately. However, if you care for your pumpkins properly there will be much less chance of any diseases.

GIANT PUMPKIN GROWING CHEAT SHEET

Most people will grow a pumpkin of ten or maybe even twenty pounds and think that is fantastic, which it is! For most people the object of the exercise is to grow pumpkins for eating or carving, but for some people they want a little bit more! They want a monster, perhaps even a competition winner, whether to show off to their friends or to gain the notoriety and fortune that comes from being a giant pumpkin grower.

This section is designed to be a cheat sheet for you, summarizing what you need to do to grow giant pumpkins. Anyone can do this, you just need some space, some seeds and some time, but you can be rewarded with a huge pumpkin! One year I carved a 118lb pumpkin (which took a lot of effort with three inch thick flesh) and placed it by my front door ... I was very popular with the kids and every parent stopped to chat about the pumpkin! Even if you aren't winning competitions, the kudos with having the biggest pumpkin on the block has to be worth it!

Preparing the Patch
For a truly monstrous pumpkin you will be preparing the growing area in the fall before you plant. A good sized area that is at the very minimum six foot square and in full sun is essential though bigger will be better. It should also be somewhere that hasn't grown pumpkins for two or even three years. Dig in plenty of compostable waste such as kitchen food scraps (not cooked food, not meat and not citrus fruit), shredded leaves, grass clippings and more. Dig this in to the whole area and leave it to sit over winter. Early spring you need to check your soil and then dig in more manure. Pumpkins are incredibly greedy feeders so the more food you can provide them then the bigger your pumpkin will get.

Sowing the Seed
Start your pumpkin seeds off indoors around the middle of April. Dills Atlantic Giant are a good variety unless you can get hold of some seeds from competition winning giant pumpkins. Plant your seeds in four inch diameter pots (peat pots or plastic) and keep the moist. Within five to seven days you should see the seeds sprouting but if they haven't by ten days then you need to re-sow.

Transplant the Seedlings

Harden off your seedlings before planting them out after the risk of frost has passed. If you have used peat pots then put the pot directly in the ground but if you have used plastic pots you need to very carefully remove the plant from the pot.

Shelter the Seedlings

To start with you can shelter your pumpkins either with a mini greenhouse or plastic cloches. The professionals use ground heating cables but the sub-urban gardener probably will not have access to these. Wind barriers can help the plants get established and protect them from extreme weather but one the plants are established and the weather has warmed both types of protection can be removed. If there is any risk of frost you should cover your pumpkin plants with cloches or horticultural fleece in order to protect them from the cold.

Keep the Weeds Down

Keep the entire pumpkin patch free from weeds as this will prevent them using the nutrients you have put in the soil and help to protect your pumpkins from insects and other diseases. Remove the weeds before they can get established.

Pollinate the Flowers

In late June or early July, depending on where you are, the flowers need to be pollinated so the pumpkins can form. This will occur naturally but more giant pumpkin growers will do it by hand to ensure it takes place and that the fruits they want to keep are pollinated. Check the section on pollination earlier for full details.

Select Your Pumpkin

Check the vines every few days to see where new pumpkins are developing and early to mid-July you will choose the two fastest growing pumpkins and remove all the rest. You will need to take daily measurements of your pumpkins so you know which are growing the best but usually they will be on the main vine. Should any more pumpkins or flowers develop these can also be removed so that all the plants energy is directed into the two pumpkins you have kept.

Caring for the Vines

You need to care for your vines as they are growing and check for pests and diseases because there are many that will damage your pumpkin. If you are vigilant then you can catch problems early on and deal with them before they damage your plants.

Feed, Fertilize and Water

Pumpkins have relatively shallow roots so need a good amount of water, particularly when it is hot. You have to water them regularly because if they go through periods of drought and watering then they can split after a growth spurt. Giant pumpkins need a LOT of water with the biggest needing as much as a hundred gallons of water in a day and they can put on anywhere from 30 to 60 pounds in a single day!

Fertilize your plants well and use a liquid kelp and fish food as it is high in micro-nutrients. Home-made compost tea is great as is molasses, humic acid and fulvic acid.

Harvesting Your Pumpkins

As the days get shorter so it is time to harvest your giant pumpkin which needs to be removed from the vine and stored indoors before the frosts hit. Moving it can be very difficult depending on the size and you will need to plan how you are going to move it very carefully to avoid damaging it. Rolling it on to a blanket or tarp is one way to move it if you have people who can help you lift it though make sure the blanket is strong enough to support the weight!

If you are growing competitively then you will leave your pumpkin on the vine literally until the last moment, often well into October.

Growing giant pumpkins takes patience and a lot of attention, but it is great fun and very rewarding. Like I said early, the ego boost from having the largest pumpkin on the block makes it well worth while!

KEEPING YOUR SEEDS FOR NEXT YEAR

When growing giant pumpkins you will typically keep the seeds from the largest one or two pumpkins and use those the following year. These seeds have proven genetics, coming from giant pumpkins and so are much more likely to produce a giant. For genetic diversity purposes you may want to grow some normal giant pumpkins such as Dills Atlantic Giant and pollinate your seeds with the Atlantic Giant seeds.

To save the seeds you have to remove the stringy pulp and the seeds from inside the pumpkin. Put this in a colander and run water over it. As the water runs over the pulp, pick out the seeds and rinse them.

There are going to be a lot more seeds that you are ever likely to plant but pick through them all and spread them out on a side when they are rinsed. You are looking for the largest seeds which you want to keep whilst the smaller seeds can be given away, sometimes sold if the pumpkin is larger enough or roasted and eaten.

Typically you would keep three or four times the number of seeds than you would need so if you are planning on growing ten pumpkin plants you would keep thirty or forty seeds. The larger seeds will have the best chance of germinating.

The rinsed seeds now need to be put on a paper towel and spaced out so they don't stick to each other. Put them somewhere cool and dry for about a week. Once the seeds are dry put them in an envelope somewhere cool and dark until you need them.

One method that seems to work is to put the pumpkin seed envelope in a plastic container, punch a few holes in the lid (to prevent condensation) and then place the container in the back of your refrigerator! However, any cool, dark place will do and I tend to store mine in the cellar which is cool, dark and has good air circulation.

When you start growing giant pumpkins you will want to keep the seeds because the championship winning growers will keep their seeds and breed giant varieties together in order to make a monster, world record beating pumpkin.

FAVORITE PUMPKIN RECIPES

No book on pumpkins would be complete without some recipes. Whilst giant pumpkins do not make the best eating, smaller pumpkins are certainly tastier and with better quality flesh, they are still usable and make for some delicious meals. I tend to end up with a freezer full of meals made out of pumpkin or just pumpkin puree which I then use throughout the year.

These are some of my favorite recipes and are truly delicious, being a fitting end for your giant pumpkin!

Pumpkin Pie

The American classic, this sweet pumpkin pie is to die for and is best served with thick fresh cream. It is pretty easy to make and will take a little over an hour to prepare and cook. You can get six servings out of this recipe though usually I only manage two or three!

Ingredients:
- 1¾ cups pumpkin puree (roast the pumpkin for about 45 minutes or until soft and then puree for the best flavour otherwise you can boil it in water)
- 1¾ cups sweetened condensed milk
- 2/3 cup light brown sugar (firmly packed)
- 2 tablespoons white sugar
- 1¼ teaspoons ground cinnamon
- ½ teaspoon salt
- ½ teaspoon ground ginger
- ½ teaspoon ground nutmeg
- ¼ teaspoon ground cloves
- 2 eggs (beaten)
- 9" pie crust (unbaked – either home-made or store bought)

Method:
1. Mix all the ingredients in a bowl and stir until thoroughly combined – use an electric mixer as it is quicker and will take just a couple of minutes
2. Pour the mixture into the pie crust
3. Bake for 15 minutes in an oven pre-heated to 425F

4. Turn the temperature down to 350F and cook for a further 50 minutes or until a knife inserted into the middle comes out clean
5. Cool on a wire rack

Pumpkin Soup

For me this is one of the main reasons for growing pumpkins and the recipe scales up nicely to produce large quantities. It can easily be made vegetarian by swapping the chicken stock for vegetable stock. By not using the butter, cheese or double cream it can be made into a perfect soup for slimmers. It takes about ninety minutes for prepare this soup and the recipe makes enough for about six servings.

Ingredients:

- 1½kg pumpkin
- 1 head of garlic (cut horizontally in half – use less garlic if you prefer)
- Handful of rosemary sprigs
- 1½ tablespoons olive oil plus extra for drizzling
- 1 onion (peeled and chopped)
- 15g butter
- 800ml chicken stock
- 100ml double cream
- 30g Parmesan
- Pinch of nutmeg

Optional Garnish:

- 400g mixed wild mushrooms (cleaned and trimmed)
- 10g butter
- 1½ tablespoons olive oil
- Parmesan shavings

Method:

1. Heat your oven to 340F/170F
2. Cut a chunk of pumpkin (smaller pumpkins can be cut in half) and remove the seeds
3. Score the flesh with a knife, season with salt and pepper then rub the flesh of the pumpkin with the garlic halves
4. Place a garlic half (or just a clove) plus some rosemary sprigs in each piece of pumpkin
5. Drizzle with some olive oil and bake for about an hour on baking trays until tender (test with a knife at the thickest part of the flesh)
6. Take off the garlic and rosemary but keep the garlic
7. Whilst it is still hot scoop out the flesh and puree in your blender
8. In a large saucepan heat the olive oil then cook the onion for about five minutes until it turns soft and translucent
9. Scoop the flesh out from two or three of the roasted garlic cloves and add it to the pan together with some salt and pepper plus the nutmeg
10. Cook for another two minutes
11. Add the pumpkin plus the Parmesan cheese then pour in the stock (leave the cheese out if you want a diet version – it still tastes fantastic)

12. Bring to the boil then simmer for ten to twelve minutes
13. Stir in the cream (omit for the diet version) and heat for a further minute)
14. Ladle the soup in batches into a blender and blend until smooth
15. Add the butter and blend again (omit the butter for the diet version)
16. Pour the soup into a fresh pan and reheat
17. For the garnish, fry the mushrooms in a pan with the olive oil for a few minutes then add the butter, season to taste and stir well before removing from the heat
18. Serve immediately (can be frozen if cream/butter hasn't been added) and garnish with the mushrooms and Parmesan shavings

Roasted Pumpkin Seeds

This is a great use for your pumpkin seeds and make for a delicious snack. I tend to make this every year though usually end up with far more seeds than I can cook! It will take you about 50 minutes to make this, though most of that time is cooking time not preparation time!

Ingredients:

- 1½ cups pumpkin seeds (remove all pulp and rinse)
- 2 teaspoons olive oil
- Salt
- Optional seasonings include garlic powder, cayenne pepper, Cajun seasoning, seasoning salt and so on

Method:

1. Preheat your oven to 300D
2. Put the seeds in a bowl with the olive oil and the seasonings (salt is essential if nothing else)
3. Toss well and then spread in a single layer on a baking sheet
4. Cook for around 45 minutes, stirring occasionally until the seeds turn a golden brown color

Pumpkin Gingerbread

Another great recipe that uses up the mountains of pumpkin you will have. This is also very delicious and makes for a lovely treat. It takes about an hour and this recipe will make two 9x5" loaves.

Ingredients:

- 15oz pumpkin puree (roast it and puree it for the best flavour)
- 4 eggs
- 3½ cups all-purpose flour
- 3 cups sugar
- 1 cup vegetable oil
- 2/3 cup water
- 2 teaspoons baking soda
- 2 teaspoons ground ginger
- 1½ teaspoons salt
- 1 teaspoon ground cloves
- 1 teaspoon ground allspice

- 1 teaspoon ground cinnamon
- ½ teaspoon baking powder

Method:
1. Preheat your oven to 350F and lightly grease two 9x5" loaf tins
2. In a large mixing bowl stir together the oil, eggs and sugar, beating until smooth.
3. Add the water and beat until thoroughly combined
4. Stir in the pumpkin puree plus the allspice, clove, cinnamon and ginger
5. In a separate bowl mix together the flour, salt, baking powder and baking soda
6. Add the dry ingredients to the wet ingredients and stir until the ingredients are mixed
7. Divide the batter equally between the two pans
8. Bake for about an hour until a toothpick inserted into the middle comes out clean

Pumpkin Hummus

A lovely treat with your pumpkin and great with pitta bread or chips. I personally enjoy this with vegetable batons (mostly home grown) such as carrots, cucumber, celery and peppers. This beans do need to sit overnight, so you need to make it in advance and the recipe should make about five cups of hummus.

Ingredients:
- 15oz pumpkin puree (roast for the best flavour)
- 5 fluid ounces lemon juice
- 3 garlic cloves (minced)
- 1¾ cups dry garbanzo beans (you can use canned so you don't have to leave the beans standing overnight)
- ½ cup tahini paste
- 1/3 cup extra-virgin olive oil
- ½ teaspoon ground nutmeg
- ½ teaspoon ground allspice
- ½ teaspoon ground cinnamon

Method:
1. Put the garbanzo beans into a large pan and cover with water, leaving to stand for eight hours. Alternatively bring the pan to the boil, turn off the heat, cover and leave for an hour
2. If you soaked the beans you then need to change the water in the pan, bring it to the boil, cover and simmer on a lower heat for up to two hours until the beans are tender
3. Refrigerate the beans and the liquid until cold
4. Drain the beans but keep the liquid
5. Put the beans and ½ cup of their juices in a blender and puree until it is smooth
6. Add the rest of the ingredients and puree again until smooth
7. Add more of the cooking liquid until you get the consistency you desire then season to taste with salt

Pumpkin Muffins

Another great treat to make from your pumpkins which make for a great snack. These muffins are one way to get kids to eat pumpkin and are not too difficult to make. It will take about 50 minutes to make these and you will get 14 muffins from the recipe.

Ingredients:

- 1 cup pumpkin puree
- 2 eggs (beaten lightly)
- 1¾ cups flour
- 1½ cups sugar
- ½ cup water
- ½ cup melted shortening
- 1 teaspoon ground cinnamon
- 1 teaspoon baking soda
- ½ teaspoon ground ginger
- ½ teaspoon ground nutmeg
- ¼ teaspoon baking powder
- ¼ teaspoon ground cloves
- ¼ teaspoon salt

Method:

1. In a large bowl blend the pumpkin, water, shortening and eggs together
2. Sift together the rest of the ingredients and stir into the pumpkin mixture
3. Fill greased muffin tins about ¾ full with this mixture
4. Bake in a pre-heated oven for around half an hour or until they are set when you touch them

ENDNOTE

Growing giant pumpkins is an incredibly rewarding hobby and there is nothing quite like seeing a pumpkin weighing several hundred pounds or more sitting in your pumpkin patch. The sense of achievement from accomplishing something like this is strong and you will feel very satisfied with yourself.

Whether you grow for competitions or for fun is entirely up to you. I know a lot of people grow just for fun so their kids can show off the giant pumpkin to all their friends at Hallowe'en. However, some people enter their pumpkins into competitions which is a great hobby. There are very specific requirements for competition pumpkins which you need to be aware off and they do vary between competitions.

However, this book has told you everything you need to know to get growing giant pumpkins. Whether you are going for the truly monstrous pumpkin or just want a big pumpkin is up to you, but it starts with seed selection and goes from there with the right soil preparation, the right feeding schedule, enough watering and more.

Don't get me wrong, growing giant pumpkins is rewarding but if you are serious about winning weigh-in competitions then you need to put in a lot of work! Some people will do this but others will do most of what is in this book and grow pumpkins that are a couple of hundred pounds (plenty big enough to impress your neighbors). If you are willing to put in the work though you can end up with a pumpkin over a thousand pounds and with the right seeds and some breeding you could be heading for a world record breaker!

You can grow giant pumpkins in your back yard today and all you need to do is select the site, prepare it and get planting. I can't recommend this hobby enough and like I said, the sense of satisfaction is immense!

Good luck with your giant pumpkin growing exploits, I'd love to see how well you do and how big you can get a pumpkin! Remember, follow everything in this book and you will have a monster that will be the pride of your kids and the envy of your neighbors!

OTHER GARDENING BOOKS BY JASON

Please check out my other gardening books on Amazon, available on Kindle and paperback.

Growing Fruit: The Complete Guide to Growing Fruit At Home

This is a complete guide to growing fruit from apricots to walnuts and everything in between. You will learn how to choose fruit plants, how to grow and care for them, how to store and preserve the fruit and much more. With recipes, advice and tips this is the perfect book for anyone who wants to learn more about growing fruit at home, whether beginner or experienced gardener.

Growing Tomatoes: Your Guide to Growing Delicious Tomatoes At Home

This is the definitive guide to growing delicious and fresh tomatoes at home. Teaching you everything from selecting seeds to planting and caring for your tomatoes as well as diagnosing problems this is the ideal book for anyone who wants to grow tomatoes at home. A comprehensive must have guide.

How to Compost – Turn Your Waste into Brown Gold

This is a complete step by step guide to making your own compost at home. Vital to any gardener, this book will explain everything from setting up your compost heap to how to ensure you get fresh compost in just a few weeks. A must have handbook for any gardener who wants their plants to benefit from home-made compost.

Hydroponics: A Beginners Guide to Growing Food without Soil

Hydroponics is growing plants without soil, which is a fantastic idea for indoor gardens. It is surprisingly easy to set up, once you know what you are doing and is significantly more productive and quicker than growing in soil. This book will tell you everything you need to know to get started growing flowers, vegetables and fruit hydroponically at home.

Straw Bale Gardening – No Dig, No Bending Productive Vegetable Gardens

This book tells you everything you want to know about the innovative method of straw bale gardening. Discover this no dig, no bend, low maintenance form of growing fruits, vegetables and flowers that is gaining a lot of attention. This book will guide you through the whole process from setting up your bales to planting and more. A complete, step by step guide to this innovating gardening method.

Vertical Gardening: Maximum Productivity, Minimum Space

This is exciting form of gardening allows you to grow large amounts of fruit and vegetables in small areas, maximizing your usage of space. Whether you have a large garden, an allotment or just a small balcony, you will be able to grow more delicious fresh produce. Find out how I grew over 70 strawberry plants in just three feet of ground space and more in this detailed guide.

Worm Farming: Creating Compost at Home with Vermiculture

Learn about this amazing way of producing high quality compost at home by recycling your kitchen waste. Worms break it down and produce a sought after, highly nutritious compost that your plants will thrive in. Not matter how big your garden you will be able to create your own worm farm and compost using the techniques in this step-by-step guide. Learn how to start worm farming and producing your own high quality compost at home.

Made in the USA
San Bernardino, CA
29 November 2015